MW01244364

# You Can Read Music: QuickStart

First lessons in understanding all of the symbols
on the page of music

By Bob Overman, M.Mus

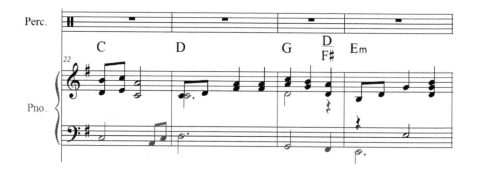

Does this look like Greek or Chinese or Algebra to you?

Don't be left in the dark!  Gain access to thousands of songs by
learning a new language to express yourself.

In this training I will show you how to understand all of this.

In just a few short lessons it will begin to make sense, and before
long it will seem natural to you.

You'll join the ranks of those who read and play music!

READ THIS FIRST!

Congratulations on taking this first step in the journey to musical literacy. This short book is written to help you decipher the symbols and the terms that you will find on a page of music.

This is a bit like learning the ABC's—once you know the name of each letter and what it sounds like, you can begin to make sense of words.

Learning to read music is a lot like learning to read your spoken language. It is going to take practice and repetition for the concepts to sink in and become part of your skill set.

So this book will teach you the ABC's, and you will have to take the next steps to move beyond simply understanding the symbols and to become a music reader.

At the end of the book I have suggestions for how to take those next steps.

For now, forge ahead and get a grip on what everything means, and how the symbols and lines work together. I cover a LOT of material in a short book, so don't expect to soak it all in at once. Come back to the parts that don't make sense at first.

By the end of this book you will have enough orientation to move ahead with confidence as you join the ranks of music readers around the world.

Let's get started!

# Table of Contents

## High and Low

Let's begin with the simplest concept in music, which is high and low.

Every sound in music can be arranged according to whether it sounds high or low to the ear.

Sounds are not actually high or low, like up in a tree or down on the ground, but humans all seem to have the same sense that sounds like the bass drum or tuba sound "low" and sounds like the triangle or the piccolo sound "high." The quality of being high or low is called 'pitch.'

*Tuning Fork*

For us to communicate about sounds, we must agree on what certain sounds should be called, based on how high or low they are. Without going into too much detail, the common agreement in western music is that the sound made by a tuning fork when it is struck (causing it to vibrate at 440 cycles per second) should be called "A".

You may be familiar with Do-Re-Mi, a simple way of naming notes as they go up in a series. We will talk about the series, or scale, a bit later, but what's important in this section is to realize that when we go up the series, presently we come to a note that sounds a lot like the one we started with—only "higher."

The Do-Re-Mi scale goes like this: Do-Re-Mi-Fa-Sol-La-Ti-Do. Notice that Do is at the beginning AND at the end. That's because we have come to a note that sounds the same, just higher. If we had started on the note called "A", we'd be back at the note "A" again, only higher. A-B-C-D-E-F-G-A.

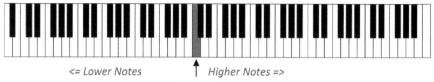

<= Lower Notes    ↑  Higher Notes =>

Middle C

You have probably seen a piano keyboard. On the piano, "low" notes are on the left end, and "high" notes are on the right end. A grand piano is longer on the left side, because low notes are produced by longer strings. This is why a stand-up bass viol, which has long strings, makes low notes, while a violin, with much shorter strings, makes high notes.

When a musician plays a guitar and presses down on the string, she is making the string shorter (at least the part that is still free to vibrate when it is plucked or strummed), and that makes the sound higher.

Here's a cool math & music fact: if you shorten the length of the string by half, you get that same sound again, only higher! If you have a string that makes an "A", then if you press in the middle you get the higher A. You can press it halfway again at the ¾ mark and get another even higher A. For math geeks, one half of the A (440) string will vibrate at 880 cycles per second, which is the next higher 'A.'

This has all been about how it sounds. But we want to read music, right? So we need to know how this looks when it is written down.

## Putting "High and Low" on Paper

Musicians have developed a way of putting the "high and low" information needed to recreate musical notes onto the written page. Music is written on a grid, with high and low written actually high and low (intuitive!). And also intuitive for those of us who read left to right, the other important element of music, which is Time, goes from left to right.

On the piano, the note in the middle is called Middle C. So let's put that Middle C on a line in the middle of a grid. You could plot music on a 45-line grid with all the notes on a piano, and that would look like this: =>

*Middle C*

This is bewildering even to a trained musician's eye. So we have learned to simplify the grid to let our eye focus on just enough information at one time.

*Staff with Treble Clef*

Instead of 45 lines, which would give us room to write all of the notes normally used in music, musicians like to use 5 lines at a time. This is easy for the eye to take in at a glance, and it's easy to see where the middle, top and bottom are. A group of 5 lines is called a Staff.

Just having 5 lines isn't enough, though, because that doesn't tell you which of the 45 possible lines they are. We need to anchor those lines somewhere. And today we use two main symbols to do that.

The first of these is called the Treble Clef ("treble" means "high", and Clef means 'key'—which in this sense means it's the key to knowing where our 5 lines fit in the grand scheme of things). The treble clef is also known

*Treble Clef & Middle C*

as the G clef, because it does its swirly thing right around the line we call G.

Remember Middle C? It lives on its own line just below the staff with a Treble Clef. A little added line like that is called a 'ledger' line. You can count up from C on the ledger line, D in the space below the staff, the E on the bottom line, F in the first space, G on the second line, and so on. Remember after G we have A again.

So going up from the bottom, the lines on the Treble Clef staff are E-G-B-D-F, and the spaces are F-A-C-E. In music lessons we remember these with mnemonics such as "Every Good Boy Does Fine". And FACE, which is cool because it's a word already.

The second Clef symbol is called the Bass Clef (you guessed it, "Bass" means "low"). Everybody knows the sound of the amplified bass in the car next to you at the stoplight. The bass clef is used for writing lower notes. It is also known as the F Clef, because it looks kind of like a cursive F, and the two little dots bracket the line with the F note below Middle C.

Once again, Middle C lives on its own ledger line, this time ABOVE the F clef staff. Same idea with lines and spaces, but this time we are counting down from middle C, to B in the space above the staff, A on the top line, G in the top space, and then F and so on.

Middle C

C D E F G A B C D E F G A B C

Counting up from the bottom of the bass clef, the lines are G-B-D-F-A (good boys deserve fudge always) and the spaces are A-C-E-G (all cows eat grass).

G B D F A

A C E G

For those who are so inclined, here is how to draw the clefs.

To draw the treble clef, start in the low F space, curve up left to the G & right up to the B, then down to the E, up to the D, start reversing and go up to the B above the first ledger line, stop, then make a VERY narrow 'S' shape downward, crossing your first mark at the D line, bisecting your first curve at the G line, then curving left again to touch the A ledger line & ending with a nice little circle right on the C ledger line. Simple! (Not. Keep trying!)

To draw the bass clef, start with a small circle on the F line, curve left slightly then right up to the A line, then down clockwise making a sort of half-valentine shape ending in the A space just below your first small circle. Finish it off with two small dots in the E and G spaces to bracket the F line.

Piano players learn to put both treble and bass clef staves together into the Grand Staff, which is used generally for the right hand in the treble clef and the left hand in the bass clef. The grand staff leaves extra room in between for other kinds of information, like song lyrics, or markings to indicate how soft or loud, or how fast or in what style to play. Piano players get used to Middle C being located both just below the treble clef and just above the bass clef, and somehow both places being the same note.

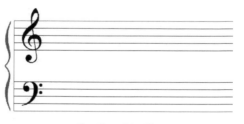
*The Grand Staff*

When notes are higher or lower than the staff, we use ledger lines to keep on going. But there are a LOT more notes up high and down

low, and after three ledger lines it starts to get hard to figure out where you are anymore. So we have a notation device that we use to indicate that the notes under it are to played in their "higher" versions. Remember the scale that went A-B-C-D-E-F-G-A?

The second A is the 8th note in the series, and the two A's are said to be an 'octave' apart ('oct-' is the Greek prefix for eight, which is why October is the eighth month...wait, what? No, which is why the octopus gets its name, as it has 8 arms).

## Written Notes       Actual Notes Played

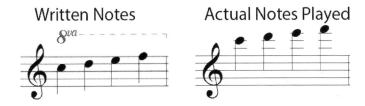

Much of our musical terminology developed in Italy, so we have lots of terms still in Italian, and here's one of them: *all'ottava* ('at the octave') is abbreviated '8va,' or *all'ottava bassa* ('at the octave lower') is '8vb'. When you see those symbols you know to play an octave higher or lower than the notes are written. And you may occasionally even see instructions to transpose TWO octaves using 15va or 15vb. This saves us from too many ledger lines.

# Time

Music is made up of notes occurring within time. How is the time element of music expressed in written form? Musical time is depicted from left to right, with time marked out in even sections,

*Measures and Bar Lines*

called 'measures,' which fall between vertical lines known as measure lines or 'bar' lines.


**'Rhythm'** is the term that describes how the regular pulses of the music, known as 'beats,' are organized.

The most common kind of rhythm in music has four regular pulses in a measure, with the first beat emphasized the most, and the third beat having a secondary emphasis:

"ONE-two-Three-four."

This would be written by having one measure with four notes in it.


*Quarter notes*

Because each of those notes is one quarter of a measure, they are called quarter notes. Quarter notes have black oval heads, and a stem about three line spaces long. Stems can go either up or down, and usually the direction is determined by where the note lands in the staff: stems go up if the note is in the bottom half, and down if in the top half. Notes on the middle line can have stems go either way. *Note (no pun intended!) that the stems go up from the right, or down from the left. NEVER the other way, like you see sometimes on coffee mugs designed by the musically untrained.* ☺

12

There are notes with longer durations. The half note, which is half of the measure (two quarter notes in duration) is written with a white or unfilled notehead and a stem; and the whole note, which is a whole measure (four quarter notes in duration), is simply an unfilled note head with no stem.

*Half Note*

**O**

*Whole Note*

Notes with shorter durations include the eighth note (there are eight of these per measure, and two of these equal one quarter note in duration) which is like a quarter note with a flag on the stem on the opposite side from the notehead; the sixteenth note (half the duration of the eighth note) with two flags. This takes care of 95% of the notes you will see. There are also thirty-second and 64th notes with three and four flags respectively, but you don't often see these before advanced levels.

*Eighth Note*

*Sixteenth Note*

When the shorter notes occur in groups their flags will be joined together, in which case they are called beams.

*Beamed Sixteenth notes*

13

Each type of note has a corresponding 'rest,' which indicates a duration of silence. Professional musicians perform the silences! The whole note rest is a small block hanging from the fourth line; the half rest is a similar small block resting on top of the middle line (like a 'hat', which

| NAME | NOTE | REST | LENGTH |
|---|---|---|---|
| Whole Note | | | 4 beats |
| Half Note | | | 2 beats |
| Quarter Note | | | 1 beat |
| Eighth Note | | | 1/2 beat |
| Sixteenth Note | | | 1/4 beat |

sounds kind of like 'half'). The quarter rest looks a little like a backward number 3, while the eighth rest looks like a forward slash with a sideways comma attached to the top, sort of a '7' shape. Sixteenth rests have two 'commas', while 32$^{nd}$ & 64$^{th}$ rests have 3 and 4.

Rests will be fitted into the measure to most clearly show where the beats fall.

What if the musical tone needs to sound longer than one of the note values? Well, we have two options:

We can add a dot to any note or rest, which adds an extra 50% to

its duration. Thus a dotted quarter note is equal to a quarter plus an eighth. Or a dotted half note is equal to a half plus a quarter.

Or, if the needed duration doesn't happen to be an extra 50% we can stick multiple notes together using a curved line known as a '**tie**' to connect them. This curve is called a 'tie' because we use it to tie notes into one longer sound. The tie is smile-shaped under notes in the lower half of the staff, and frown-shaped above notes in the upper half of the staff.

*2 beats + 1 beat = 3 beats*

Ties can't be used to connect notes of different pitches. For that the '**slur**' is used, and a slur can connect two notes or many into one group, called a 'phrase.' Slurs often indicate the group of notes should be played in one breath for wind instruments, or one bow-stroke for string instruments. Slurs have similar shapes to ties, but can be much wider, sometimes crossing over multiple measures.

Slurs are used in vocal and choral music to indicate that a single text syllable is sung over the course of several notes. This example is from 'Angels We Have Heard on High,' a favorite Christmas carol:

## Meter

We have spoken of the common kind of meter already, which is music with four beats to the measure. Normally the quarter note gets the beat, and in this common meter there are four quarter notes in the measure. Musicians need to know the meter of the music before they start playing, so there is a symbol given right at the start.

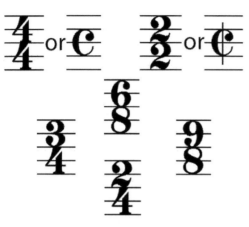

Frequently Used Time Signatures

In the first measure, after the clef symbol (and after the **key signature**, which is explained later), the Time Signature is given. This is normally two numbers, one over the other—but it's not a fraction. The top number tells how many beats in the measure, and the bottom number tells what kind of note value gets the beat. So in 4/4 time, there are four beats, each represented by a quarter note. This is called Common Meter, and can be indicated by a large letter C for 'Common.' Most popular music is in common meter. Waltzes are in triple meter, three beats to the bar, so they have a time signature of ¾.

Another time signature that occurs often is 2/2, two beats per measure, each beat represented by a half note. This is also called "Cut Time" and can be indicated by a large letter C with a line down through it, which looks like a big 'cents' symbol.

Also fairly common is 6/8, which is a little bit different in that while there are six beats per measure and the eighth note gets the beat, this really has a feeling of two larger beats each of three eighth notes' duration. So the main pulse really feels like a dotted quarter note: One-a-la Two-a-la. Another similar time signature is 9/8, which is played as three groups of three. Time Signatures based on groups of three are known as Compound Meters.

Most music has one time signature at the beginning, but some music changes time signatures as it goes along, maybe even every measure! The musicians must count carefully in such pieces.

## Tempo

The word 'tempo' refers to the speed of the music. There is a whole range of possible speeds, from slow & dirge-like to crazy fast. The Italian terms are still frequently used, so here is a chart that shows the relative speeds from slow to fast. These terms are all relative rather than precise. If the composer is particular about the exact tempo, a metronome marking can be used (a metronome is a mechanical or electronic device that clicks at a chosen rate in beats per minute). The metronome marking indicates the note value and how many per minute.

That looks like this:

*Metronome Marking*

## TEMPO TERMS TABLE

| SLOW | Grave | Extremely slow and solemn |
|---|---|---|
| | Adagio | Very slow |
| | Lento | Slow |
| | Largo | Slow and broad |
| | Larghetto | Less slow than Largo |
| MEDIUM | Andante | Rather slow, moderate walking pace |
| | Andantino | A little faster than Andante |
| | Moderato | Moderate pace |
| | Allegretto | Fairly quick, slightly slower than Allegro |
| FAST | Con moto | With movement or quickness |
| | Allegro | Lively, rather quick |
| | Vivace | Quick and lively |
| | Presto | Very quick |
| | Prestissimo | As quick as possible |

Sometimes the music changes in tempo. Different sections of longer pieces may each have different tempo markings. And tempo can also vary within a piece: *accelerando* means getting quicker, *meno mosso* means with less movement, or slower, *ritardando* means getting slower, *rallentando* means getting much slower.

Sometimes music comes to a pause, often indicated by a *fermata*. The *fermata* means the note is held for an unspecified length of time (often half again as long as the indicated note value).

*Fermata*

## Scales & Key Signatures

When we sing Do-Re-Mi-Fa-Sol-La-Ti-Do we are singing what is known as a major scale. A scale is a pattern of steps. Steps can be either half-steps (notes right next to each other on the piano keyboard) or whole steps (notes separated by an intervening note).

A Major Scale, which is often associated with happy or energetic moods, always has this pattern: whole step, whole step, half step, whole, whole, whole, half.

Let's go back to our friend Middle C. Starting on Middle C, the Major Scale is played on just the white keys: C-D-E-F-G-A-B-C.

A Minor Scale, which is often associated with sombre, sad or troubled moods, has this pattern of steps: whole-half-whole-whole-half-whole-whole. Starting on the A below middle C, the Minor Scale is played on the white keys: A-B-C-D-E-F-G-A.

What happens if we want to play our major scale starting on a different note? There are lots of reasons to choose a different starting note for the scale—perhaps the melody is a little high or low if you start on C. So you might want to start on D, for example.

But if you start on D and follow the step pattern for the major scale, the first whole step takes you to E, and the second takes you to the black key between F & G. This is a problem in terms of writing that note down, because we don't have anywhere to put that note: F is on the space and G is on the next line. The solution is to use the Sharp symbol, which indicates that the F should be played on the next black key up. (We don't need the F key in the Major Scale starting on D, so this works out just fine.) We also discover as we continue that our pattern requires the C to be a C# also.

*D Major key signature*

Rather than writing a # on every F and every C in the whole piece, musicians have learned to write them at the left edge of each line of music, immediately after the clef symbol. This shorthand is called the **Key Signature**. Music written in the major scale starting on D is said to be 'in the key of D,' and the Key Signature of D is two sharps, F# and C#.

If we start the major scale on F we have a different problem. "Whole, whole, half" brings us to the black key below B. Now we have to use the Flat Symbol, which lowers the note one half-step. So the key signature of F major is one flat (Bb).

*Flat symbol*

Don't panic, but there is a different key signature for the major scale on every single note in the octave, including the black keys. And to make matters worse, some of the black keys go by two names! (A half-step up from C is C-sharp, and a half-step down from D is D-flat...but C-sharp and D-flat are the same note!) So the major scale starting on C#, which has seven sharps in its key signature—sounds identical to the major scale on Db (the same note on the piano!) which has five flats.

### Key Signatures: Major and Relative Minor

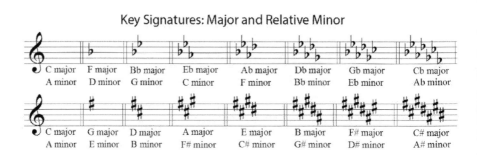

| C major | F major | Bb major | Eb major | Ab major | Db major | Gb major | Cb major |
| A minor | D minor | G minor | C minor | F minor | Bb minor | Eb minor | Ab minor |

| C major | G major | D major | A major | E major | B major | F# major | C# major |
| A minor | E minor | B minor | F# minor | C# minor | G# minor | D# minor | A# minor |

And remember the minor scale? Yep, a different key signature for each minor scale as well. But here's some good news: C major and A minor had no sharps or flats (together referred to as 'accidentals').

Because they share the same key signature, they are called 'relative' scales—the 'relative major' of A minor is C major, and the relative minor of C major is A minor. Every major scale has a relative minor (which starts on the sixth note of the major scale). So musicians only have to learn 15 key signatures, not 30.

To effectively read music it is important to have a firm grasp on the concept of keys, even if you don't learn all of the key signatures to start with. Later on, to become a really good player, it's important to master playing the major and minor scales in all of the keys.

This can seem tedious, and is one reason not everyone sticks to music lessons, but the freedom to play music in any key is worth the effort.

Sometimes in a melody we need to play one of the notes that isn't in the scale, and to do that we might need to cancel the sharp or the flat. To do that we use a Natural. Or we might use a sharp or flat temporarily. When we use these

*Natural*

symbols inside of a measure instead of in the key signature, the effect is cancelled by the next bar line. And sometimes in more advanced music we may need to raise or lower a note even further than ½ step, so we may use a double sharp or a double flat.

# Dynamics

Music can be loud or soft, and there are many words to describe volume and changes in volume. The table below shows the most common terms used to instruct musicians to play soft or loud. Once again we are using Italian terms.

## DYNAMIC MARKING TERMS AND SYMBOLS

| Italian term | Musical symbol | Meaning |
|---|---|---|
| Pianissimo | *pp* | Very soft |
| Piano | *p* | Soft |
| Mezzopiano | *mp* | Moderately soft |
| Mezzoforte | *mf* | Moderately loud |
| Forte | *f* | Loud |
| Fortissimo | *ff* | Very Loud |

*Changes* in volume can create some of the strongest emotional responses in the listener, and there are several common instructions for making these changes:

## DYNAMIC CHANGE TERMS AND SYMBOLS

| Crescendo | cresc. | Gradually louder |
|---|---|---|
| Decrescendo | decresc. | Gradually softer |
| Diminuendo | dim. | Gradually softer |
| Sforzando | *sfz* | Strongly accented |
| Forte-piano | *fp* | Loud, then immediately soft |

# Navigation

Finding your way around in a piece of music, also known as a 'score,' can be daunting at first. The signposts are all there, but they may not be familiar, and often not in English.

Here are some of the most common symbols to help musicians know where to go next:

## Repeats

Music often has sections that are played more than once. To save paper, ink, & copyist labor, we use the same section of the score over again. But how do we signal that this is happening?

 The Open Repeat (or Start Repeat) symbol is two dots to the right of a double bar. This symbol alerts the player that this location is the spot to come back to and play again. Once past this symbol, the player will be looking for the signal to go back.

There are several ways to instruct players to return & play the section again.

The simplest is the End Repeat symbol, mirror image of the Open Repeat symbol. This simply means 'go back and play the section again.' (You don't need  an Open Repeat If you are going back to the beginning of the song.) When you come to this symbol the second time you ignore it and carry on past.

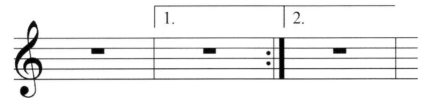

Next, and somewhat more complex, are numbered endings. These are indicated by a numbered bracket above the score, which terminates at an end repeat. The player goes back to the open repeat mark and plays the section again. However, this time the player skips the section under the first ending bracket and plays the second ending. A composer or arranger can put multiple endings in the score, and multiple numbers under any ending bracket. Each time the player comes back to the endings she plays the next one, until there is an ending with no end repeat symbol, and then she carries on past.

## The Sign (Segno)

The 'sign' (which is what *segno* means) is another way to send players back to repeat a section. The Segno is placed at the spot to return to, and instead of an end repeat, the abbreviation D.S. (for *dal segno*, "from the sign") tells the player to go back to the sign.

*Segno*

*Coda*

Variations on D.S. include *D.S. al Fine* (which means go back to the sign and play until the end mark (*Fine*) is encountered; and *D.S. al Coda* which means go back to the sign and then watch for the Jump-to-the Coda symbol, at which point you jump to the Coda ("tail"), normally a short passage at the end that brings the piece to a close.

D.C. stands for *Da Capo* ("To the head") and means go back to the very beginning. It may also be combined with other terms, like *D.C. al Fine*, or *D.C. al Coda*.

## Next Steps

In these few pages we have covered a LOT of material, which musicians spend years mastering. I hope that you are intrigued rather than overwhelmed, and that this quick overview has helped you gain some understanding of the written score, so that it begins to make sense. With practice, just like reading books, your fluency in reading music will steadily improve.

If you are eager to learn more, you could sign up for a course at your local community college, or engage a music teacher for private lessons. If you'd like a more economical approach that lets you work at your own pace, I have a series of videos coming out that go more in-depth on each topic. To get more information about the video series, visit this web page:

https://youcanreadmusic.convertri.com/course-optin

People who take the video course will also have an option to have coaching and guided practice sessions, which will be made available on our membership site.

So whether you continue your journey on your own, or I can be a part of your next steps, I extend my best wishes in your musical adventures!

Your purchase of this book gives you a deep discount on the Kindle version if you'd like to have that or give it to a friend. And please visit Amazon and leave a 5-star review if you are willing—that helps more than you know.  Thanks!

Made in the USA
Middletown, DE
07 January 2023